BEST of British

A Collection of BRITISH GREATS

First published in the UK in 2012 by Instinctive Product Development

© Instinctive Product Development 2012

www.instinctivepd.com

Printed in China

ISBN: 978-1-908816-48-1

Designed by: BrainWave

Creative Director: Kevin Gardner

Written by: David Curnock

Images courtesy of PA Photos, Shutterstock and Wiki Commons

Introduction

The British are known around the world for their distinctive and wide-ranging cultures and traditions. Many objects, products and brands are also recognisable as having their origins here in the British Isles. Our best-loved, and jealously-guarded, customs and traditions have endured the passage of time: from the humble game of conkers, to Morris dancing, football and cricket, all of these are identified as belonging to Britain. Well-loved rituals such as afternoon tea, drinking real ale and going to the pub are typical activities that are carried out by many of our people and are almost unique to our country. Our passion for fish and chips, and the Sunday roast, can be seen wherever British people gather, be it at home or overseas.

A host of engineering, manufacturing and design innovations as diverse as the television, the hovercraft and the cat's eye, owe their existence to the ingenuity and design skills of our engineers. All of these, and many more, are celebrated in this bookazine as a miscellany of things that can truly be called the **Best of British**.

John Bull:

Character created by satirist John Arbuthnot (1667-1735).

First drawn by cartoonist James Gillray (1756-1815).

In prominent use between 1880-1950s.

His well-fed proportions represented prosperity in an age where rosy cheeks and plump faces were a sign of good health.

Surname is the believed origin of the French term for the British as *les rosbifs* (the 'roast beefs').

John Bull and the English Bulldog

Often used as a symbol representing Britishness, the character John Bull dates back to the 17th century. In cartoons of the day, wearing a frock coat, buff-coloured waistcoat, white breeches and a shallow-crowned top hat, the character was typified as a country dweller of middle-class stock. His coat became royal blue in Georgian times and his traditional Union Flag waistcoat followed later.

Epitomising the British spirit, John Bull is used to encourage the nation in difficult times. Often portrayed together with an English Bulldog, the call for Britons to show the 'John Bull Spirit' has been used in times of conflict and difficulty. Representing the strength of character, fortitude and stubborn traits that are typical of the people of Britain, the image of John Bull has been used in many advertising campaigns and as part of a trademark on some British products, leaving prospective purchasers in no doubt as to their origin.

The distinctive English Bulldog was originally known as the *Bondogge* or *Bolddogge*. The name Bulldog came about when it was used in bull baiting. Nowadays this fierce-looking animal is known for being a loyal and docile family pet.

3

English Bulldog:

Descended from the Asian Mastiff.

Bred for bull-baiting in the 13th century.

Crossed with Pug dog to become a docile family pet.

Life span: 6.5 years (average).

Weight: 50-55 pounds (22.6-24.9 kilos).

Height: 12-14 inches (30.5-35.6 cm).

JOHN BULL taking a Luncheon: — or — British Cooks, cramming Old Grumble-Gizzard with Bonne Chère.

The Red Telephone Box

Along with the red London bus and the red post box, the red telephone box is an instantly recognised feature of the British landscape. A design competition sponsored by the Post Office in 1924 was won by Sir Giles Gilbert Scott, whose iconic K2 cast iron telephone box first appeared on the streets of London in 1926. The K2 was massive, being almost 10 feet (3m) tall and weighing over 1 ton (0.9 tonne) and was used almost exclusively in the capital. In all, only 1500 K2-type boxes were produced and very few remain in use today. The colour red was chosen because it made the box easy to spot.

Its successor, the widely used K6 telephone box was introduced in 1935, again designed by Scott. This design was smaller and lighter than its predecessor, weighing around 25% less, although it was still made from cast iron and painted in the same red colour. This version was used nationwide, with over 70,000 K6 boxes in use by the 1980s. One common feature of the red telephone box was the use of a Tudor crown, sometimes in gold colour, on all four sides of the domed roof section. From 1955 this crown was replaced by the St Edward's Crown or, in Scotland, the Crown of Scotland, and is an easy means of dating the K6 box.

The word 'Telephone' was written on each side of the box, on a glass panel that was internally illuminated at night. Another feature was the self-closing, outward-opening door that offered both a measure of privacy for the user and protection from the elements. The interior was originally fitted with a coin box and a shelf for a telephone directory, the latter was often found very dog-eared, if it hadn't been totally removed for some reason! By the mid-1980s, newer designs began to replace the K6 in an attempt to reduce damage by vandalism. However, around 2,000 were declared 'listed buildings' and retained in use, albeit with modern equipment installed.

■ **RIGHT: The days of spotting a telephone box in the middle of nowhere are long gone as modern mobile phones have taken their place.**

Red Telephone Box:

Designer: Sir Giles Gilbert Scott (1880-1960) who was also the architect of Liverpool Cathedral.

K2 box introduced in 1926 replacing the K1 series.

K6 box introduced in 1935 was also known as the Jubilee Kiosk to commemorate the Silver Jubilee of King George V.

Shakespeare

The name William Shakespeare can have differing effects on those who know of him. To most, he was probably the world's greatest dramatist and writer in the English language, to others, particularly students, the name fills them with trepidation as they struggle to analyse his works. Known as the 'Bard of Avon', Shakespeare's plays have been performed more often than those of any other playwright and have been translated into every major language.

Born the third of eight children, the prolific Shakespeare, originally an actor and players' company owner, became a British literary icon as a writer of plays including: *A Midsummer Night's Dream, Hamlet, Macbeth, King Lear, Merchant of Venice* and *Romeo and Juliet.* These plays are sometimes staged at the replica old Shakespeare's Globe Theatre in London.

On his gravestone is inscribed his own dramatic message:

Good frend for Iesvs sake forbeare,
To digg the dvst enclosed heare.
Bleste be ye man yt spares thes stones,
And cvrst be he yt moves my bones.
(Modern version:)
Good friend, for Jesus' sake forbear,
To dig the dust enclosed here.
Blessed be the man that spares these stones,
And cursed be he that moves my bones.

William Shakespeare:

Born: 1564.
Died: 23 April 1616, aged 52.
Married: Anne Hathaway when he was 18 years old.
Children: Susanna and twins Hamnet & Judith.
Wrote: 38 plays, 154 sonnets and many poems.
Buried: Holy Trinity Church, Stratford-upon-Avon.

British Airways

Since the creation of British Airways (BA) in 1974 out of the merger between British Overseas Airways Corporation (BOAC) and British European Airways (BEA) the airline has maintained its position in the forefront of commercial aviation. Once described as 'The World's Favourite Airline', BA was the world's first airline to fly a supersonic passenger service in 1976 when it operated Concorde on a London to Bahrain service. Sadly, it also flew the last supersonic service, from New York's JFK to London Heathrow, some 27 years later.

Apart from a period when it operated a so-called 'World Tails' scheme on its aircraft, BA has always flown a stylised Union Flag on the fin of its aircraft, leaving no doubt about the country of origin of the airline. BA operates over 220 aircraft, including 55 Boeing 747-400s, being the largest operator of that type. Its routes span the world, representing British airline interests on all six continents, serving around 150 destinations. BA dominates Heathrow airport, owning around 40% of the available slots.

British Airways:

Established: 1974.

Subsidiaries: BA CityFlyer and British Airways Helicopters, British Airways World Cargo, OpenSkies.

Franchises: Comair (South Africa) and Sun Air of Scandinavia (Denmark).

Shareholdings: Flybe (15%), InterCapital and Regional Rail, a holding company for Eurostar UK Ltd (10%).

Fortnum & Mason, Harrods and Savile Row

Fortnum & Mason, generally known as 'Fortnum's', is a typically British department store situated in central London. Established at 181 Piccadilly in 1707 by William Fortnum and Hugh Mason, the store has become recognised internationally for its high-quality goods. Having received many Royal Warrants, Fortnum's is also known as 'The Royal Grocer'. Renowned for stocking exclusive and exotic products, Fortnum's is famed for its loose-leaf tea and luxury picnic hampers. Curiously, in 1886, it was the first store in Britain to stock Heinz Baked Beans. In 1964 its then owner, W Garfield Weston, commissioned a clock in commemoration of the founders. This has become the centre of attention when, on the hour, 4-foot-tall (1.2m) models of Mr Fortnum and Mr Mason emerge and bow to each other while the chimes sound and music plays.

Harrods is an upmarket department store in Brompton Road, London. Founded in 1824 by Charles Henry Harrod in Southwark, the store moved to its current location in 1851. With 330 departments, including 32 restaurants, and staffed by over 5,000, Harrods is famous for its rich and famous clientele. The store has operated a strict dress code that has excluded uniformed soldiers, scouts and a football team, FC Shakhtar Donetsk, wearing tracksuits. Its banking department offers services that include the sale of gold bars and coins.

Savile Row has a worldwide reputation for excellence in bespoke tailoring. Many have followed the likes of Beau Brummel, who was one of the first to wear clothes made in Savile Row in 1803. Famous for its military tailors Gieves and Hawkes, this prestige address has become the location of many of the world's finest bespoke tailors and designers. To maintain a high standard, members of the Savile Row Bespoke Association must put at least 50 hours of hand labour into every two-piece suit they produce.

Fortnum & Mason:

Hampers: From around £35 to £25,000.

Tea: More than 100 exclusive loose-leaf blends from China, India, Sri Lanka and Cornwall (very rare).

Products: Include fresh poultry, ready-to-eat game in aspic jelly, quails eggs, smoked salmon.

Harrods:

Site: 5 acres (20,000m²).

Sales area: 1 + million ft² (90,000 m²).

Staff: Over 5,000 from around 50 countries.

Clients: Up to 300,000 on busy days.

■ **ABOVE:** A mainstay of London's shopping scene since 1824.

■ **RIGHT:** The world famous Harrods food hall, 1974.

Savile Row Tailors and Clients:

Davies and Son (Est. 1803) – Sir Robert Peel's police force, Harry S Truman, Michael Jackson, Calvin Klein.

Hardy Amies (Est. 1946) – HM Queen Elizabeth II.

Dege & Skinner (Est. 1865) – The King of Bahrain, The Sultan of Oman.

Nutters of Savile Row (Est.1969) – The Duke of Bedford, Bianca & Mick Jagger, The Beatles.

■ **ABOVE:** Savile Row in central London, a shopping street famous for its traditional men's tailoring.

Pubs and Real Ale

Pubs, otherwise known as public houses, are drinking establishments deeply rooted in the culture of Britain. The diarist Samuel Pepys once described the pub as 'the heart of England'. In most communities, the pub is considered the focal point, with many and varied activities apart from the actual consumption of alcoholic beverages. Traditional pubs have gradually disappeared to a point where many villages no longer have one and, in many towns and cities, they have been replaced by chain establishments that are open all day, offering food, drinks and music.

Pubs originated as 'taverns' in Roman times: later, Anglo-Saxons established roadside alehouses in their dwellings. The 'alewife' would put a green bush up on a pole outside to let people know her brew was ready. *Ye Olde Fighting Cocks* in St Albans, Hertfordshire, holds the Guinness World Record as the oldest pub in England, being an 11th-century structure on an 8th-century site. The National Trust owns 36 public houses of historic interest including the George Inn, Southwark, London, and The Crown Liquor Saloon, Belfast, Northern Ireland.

In traditional pubs, the 'landlord', being the licensee of the pub, serves his clients in the public bar, lounge bar, snug or ladies room with a range of beers, lagers, ciders, wines and spirits.

Real Ale, otherwise 'Cask Ale' is used to describe beer that is 'conditioned', and served from

Pubs:

Numbers: From 69,000 (in 1980) down to 52,000 (2010).

Most popular names: Red Lion, Royal Oak, White Hart, Rose and Crown, King's Head, Queen's Head.

Longest pub name: In Stalybridge, Cheshire – *The Old Thirteenth Cheshire Astley Volunteer Rifleman Corps Inn*.

Shortest pub name: Also in Stalybridge – *Q*.

Licensing laws: Opening hours were restricted in 1915 to stop factory workers turning up drunk thereby harming the war effort.

■ **ABOVE: The King's Head is one of the most popular pub names in Britain.**

■ **BELOW: An interior of a traditional English pub.**

■ ABOVE: The number of drinkers trying real ale for the first time has increased by 40% in the past few years, while 200 new breweries have opened.

a cask (or bottle) without the addition of carbon dioxide or nitrogen pressure. Conditioning is the secondary fermentation process. Cask ale is drawn from its cask in the cellar and piped to the bar, using a hand pump that has a stroke of around either 1/4 or 1/2 pint (0.14 or 0.28 litre). Many arguments rage over the correct way to dispense a cask ale: devotees in the North generally prefer their ale served though a 'swan neck' on the pump that creates a fuller, frothier head on their pint which is perceived as being less bitter, whereas others swear that real ale should not have a large head and thus be 'harder' in the mouth. Some, more traditional pubs have a 'tap room', where the ale is dispensed simply through a gravity tap without any pumping.

Real Ale:

Cask marque: Voluntary accreditation scheme that ensures quality of ale served.

Beer engine: The hand pump at the bar.

Draught beer: Beer drawn from a keg under gas pressure.

Microbrewery: A small brewery specialising in production of cask-conditioned ale, often brewed in small batches.

Hackney Cabs:

Makes: Beardmore Marks I to VII, Austin FX3, Carbodies/LTI FX4 & Fairway, Metrocab, LTI TX1, TXII & TX4.

Private users: HRH Prince Philip, Governor of Falkland Islands, Stephen Fry, Yvette Fielding (ex-*Blue Peter* presenter).

First advertising carried: For the London pub, *The Samuel Pepys*.

Original fare (motor cab): 8 pence for the first mile (1907).

The Knowledge: Takes an average of 12 test attempts, over a period of nearly 3 years.

No of cabs: Over 20,000 licensed in London alone; Luton has highest number per head of population.

Hackney Cabs

The origin of the term 'hackney cab' is debatable: some believe it to be a corruption of the French word *hacquenée*, meaning a horse for hire, while others claim it originated in the village of Hackney, in the east of London. Whatever its origin, the hackney cab has become an icon in the British way of life, especially in the larger cities. Records show that the first 'cab rank' was established in 1634 in the Strand, London. By 1760 there were over a thousand of the so-called 'hackney hell carts' on the streets of the capital. The word 'cab' derives from the rather elegant and speedy two-wheeled cabriolet carriage of the 1820s, while a larger four-wheeled carriage, the growler, plied for trade at railway stations.

The advent of the motorcar saw an inevitable shift away from horses: the first purpose-built cabs were electrically powered, and the first motor cab appeared in 1901. In 1919, the Beardmore company in Glasgow produced their new 'taxicab' that had excellent ride qualities. Called taxicab because of the taximeter, which was introduced by law in 1907, this was the predecessor of the hackney cab as we know it today. The taximeter calculates fares based on distance travelled and time taken, including, rather annoyingly, when stuck in traffic.

Most cabs were originally black: this was not mandatory but simply because they were only made in that colour, as for the Austin FX3. Nowadays they are often painted in different colours for advertising purposes, thus earning some extra money for the owner. Generally referred to as the London taxi, or black cab, these vehicles are to be seen all over Britain and in British territories overseas. Black cabs by law must have a turning circle of only 25ft (8m). This came about because of the size of the roundabout at the Savoy Hotel entrance.

London cab drivers have to pass a test called 'The Knowledge' to prove they have an intimate and detailed knowledge of its streets and points of interest.

■ **LEFT:** A London black cab on Regent Street decorated in preparation to celebrate the Royal Wedding.

Marmite:

Invented: 1907, in Burton-on-Trent, Staffordshire.

Ingredients: Yeast extract, salt, vegetable extract, niacin, thiamin, celery, folic acid, vitamins B12.

Made by: Unilever.

Marmite, Tartan and Scotch Whisky

Marmite has established its place in Britain's food heritage since its invention in 1907. Its name derives from a very un-British source, a French casserole dish, as depicted on the label of its jar, which has retained the same distinctive shape since the 1920s. Many British homes, especially those with children, will have a jar of this sticky, brown-coloured, yeast-based spread in their food cupboard. Opinions are strongly divided over its taste: an advertising campaign summarised this, succinctly: 'You either love it, or hate it'.

Usually eaten as a spread on toast, Marmite is sought after by ex-pat British all over the world. Another advertising campaign labelled the product 'My Mate' (Marmite): this has been taken up by the company, on its label for jars exported to Australia, to compete with their Vegemite product.

Tartan is recognised as being typically British, or more specifically, Scottish, in origin. The term is generally associated with a pattern of criss-crossed horizontal and vertical bands of multiple colours, usually of woven wool.

Tartan:

Earliest tartan: Falkirk tartan from 3rd-century AD – a simple check of natural light and dark wools.

Modern checked tartan: First seen around late 17th century.

Regional tartans: First appeared around 1703.

Different patterns: Called 'setts' around 7,000 (but only approx. 3,500 are officially recognised).

It can be found today in a variety of materials and is regarded as being almost timeless in character. The word 'tartan' is thought to be derived from the French word *tiretain*, which relates to woven cloth. Tartan material was not always patterned: in the 1830s it was said to be '…plain coloured… without pattern'. Today, most expect it to be strongly patterned, often

■ **RIGHT:** One of 60 decanters of Diamond Jubilee by John Walker & Sons Blended Scotch Whisky. It marks 60 years to the day since the Queen's accession, at Royal Lochnagar Distillery.

Scotch Whisky:

The law: It is illegal to label any whisky not distilled in Scotland as Scotch whisky.

Vatted or pure malt: Since November 2009 no whisky can be labelled with these terms; instead they are classified as blended malt (which includes Johnny Walker Green label).

Distilleries: More than half of these are in Speyside; others are in Lowland, Highland, Campbeltown and Islay. Island distilleries are classified with the Highland group.

in the colours of Scottish regions or clans. Banned in 1746, in an attempt to bring under control the Highland warrior clans who wore it, this Dress Act was repealed in 1782. Since then, it has become the symbolic national dress of Scotland.

Scotch Whisky is probably the most famous generic 'brand' in the world. Wherever people speak of, or order, a whisky they most commonly refer to it as 'Scotch'. This part of Britain has been associated with the manufacture of fine whisky since the middle of the 13th century, when a friar at Lindores Abbey, Fife, named John Cor was recorded, in the Exchequer Rolls of Scotland, as distilling it. There are five distinct types of Scotch whisky, each of which must be aged in oak barrels for at least three years: single malt; single grain; blended malt (formerly 'vatted' or 'pure' malt); blended grain; and blended Scotch whisky. The word 'single' refers to a single distillery, while 'blended' means from two or more different distilleries.

15

The Routemaster Bus

The Routemaster bus is instantly recognisable as being British. With its bright red colour and box-like appearance it has transported many millions of passengers since first appearing on the streets in 1956. This somewhat antiquated shape developed out of a functional requirement to carry a large number of passengers. With 64 seats, its double-deck layout featured an open, rear platform that allowed for a rapid entry and exit by its passengers. With a separate, enclosed cab for the driver, fares were collected by a conductor who walked through the central aisle on both decks. Fare dodging was commonplace in busy periods, as some of the more agile of its passengers leaped on and then off again before the frustrated conductor could take their fare. Although mainly associated with London Transport, the Routemaster also appeared briefly on the streets of Nottingham in 2008

Around 3,000 Routemasters were built. The 1000th example of the type, *RM1000*, was delivered in 1961 and continued in service until 1985; two years later, it was acquired by the *RM1000* preservation group at Southall. This bus now appears at transport rallies and other events proudly bearing its placard, *The 1000th Routemaster*, beneath the upper deck windows. Many of the type still survive; among these, several are used on what are known as Heritage routes in London. Some of the other survivors are used in a variety of ways, including sightseeing tour buses in Britain and around the world, wedding and party hire, grandstands at some sporting events, and as roadside cafés and restaurants.

Routemaster Bus:

Number built: Around 3,000.

Engine: AEC or Leyland 6-cylinder diesel.

Transmission: Automatic.

Bodywork: Lightweight aluminium unitary construction, made by Park Royal.

In service: 1956 to 2005 (some remain on Heritage routes).

Superseded by: New Bus For London (NB4L) in February 2012 – commonly called the New Routemaster or the BorisBus after the Mayor of London, Boris Johnson.

Some are in individual private use as motorhomes with all manner of home comforts installed, although the rear platform is usually closed in. On the 50th anniversary of the Routemaster's entry into service, over 100 preserved examples took part in a rally at Finsbury Park, London.

In 2004, the bus dealer Ensignbus held a raffle to dispose of 32 Routemasters, for the not unreasonable sum of £2,000, to those who could prove that they had the facilities, and finances, to look after them. Its replacement, the NB4L (New Bus For London), entered limited service in February 2012, again featuring the classic open rear platform.

17

■ BELOW: *RML903*, one of London's doubledecker Routemaster buses, is swung aboard the Cunard cargo liner *Alaunia* at King George V Dock, London, for a month's visit to Philadelphia, where it took part in the Exposition Britannia, 1963.

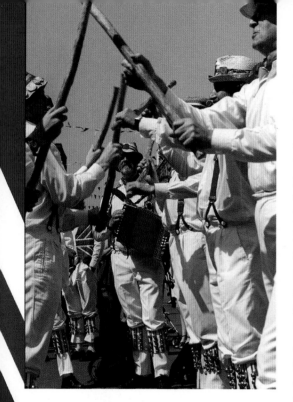

Morris Dancing and Sherlock Holmes

Morris dancing is a form of traditional English folk dance performed by groups of men or women known as sides or teams. Dating back to the late 15th century, it may have been named after the custom of dancers painting their faces black, representing the Moors of North Africa, hence 'Moor-ish' leading to the term 'Morris'. Traditionally danced in May, and on Boxing Day and other festivals, it has several forms according to whichever part of the country it is being performed. The main variations include Cotswold, North West, Border (from the England/Wales border area), Longsword and Rapper (short sword) in the North, and Molly in East Anglia.

Morris dancing is a lively, rhythmic, stepping dance carried out to the accompaniment of music. Originally, this was to tabor or drumbeats, later, to the pipe, fiddle and accordion. Dancers often wear white clothes with brightly coloured baldricks or cross-belts, with bells attached to their legs, and clogs on their feet; dress and equipment vary regionally. Carrying sticks and handkerchiefs, the sides of usually six or eight dancers shake the handkerchiefs and bang the sticks together as they dance.

Sherlock Holmes is a classic British fictional character created by the Scottish writer Sir Arthur Conan Doyle. Holmes is presented as a London-based consulting detective with his offices and lodgings, famously, at 221b Baker Street. Created in 1887, the character Holmes was inspired

■ **ABOVE: Morris dancers at the Mayday celebrations in Rochester, Kent.**

Morris Dancing:

Earliest recorded: 1448.

Longest Morris dance: In 1600, William Kemp Morris danced from London to Norwich.

Bedlam Morris: Danced with sticks, from Welsh borders across to Buckinghamshire.

Mumming plays: Often acted out by Morris sides, particularly around Christmas and New Year.

■ **ABOVE LEFT:** Sir Arthur Conan Doyle, author (1859-1930).

■ **ABOVE RIGHT:** Basil Rathbone, right, as Sherlock Holmes, and Nigel Bruce, as Dr Watson, 1945.

■ **BELOW:** Star of the recent BBC adaptation Benedict Cumberbatch.

Sherlock Holmes:

Appeared in: Four novels and 56 short stories.

Novels: *A Study in Scarlet* (in *Beeton's Christmas Annual*) – 1887; *The Sign of the Four* – 1890; *The Hound of the Baskervilles* – 1901-02 (serialised); *The Valley of Fear* – 1914-15 (serialised).

Arch-enemy: Professor Moriarty in *The Adventure of the Empty House*.

Character traits: Habitually used cocaine to stimulate his brain when not working on a case.

by Dr Joseph Bell, of Edinburgh Royal Infirmary, for whom Conan Doyle worked as a clerk. Further influences were taken from Sir Henry Littlejohn, a forensic medicine and public health lecturer at the Infirmary.

Holmes's friend and assistant, Dr John H Watson, shared his residence before and after Watson's marriage. Watson chronicled Holmes's cases and acted variously as lookout, decoy and messenger. The oft-quoted remark, 'Elementary, my dear Watson' never actually appeared in any of the Holmes stories. Known for his powers of deduction, Sherlock Holmes is, according to *The Guinness World Records,* the 'most portrayed movie character' with 75 different actors playing him in over 211 films.

Old School Tie, Scouts and the Virgin Group

The Old School Tie is an expression often used to describe the use of public school or college connections in business, or socially, among ex-pupils. Privately educated British schoolboys are known as 'old boys' after leaving. This 'old boy network' is often used to further their careers, particularly in the British Civil Service and large business corporations. The term 'It's not what you know, it's who you know' is often used to describe the benefits of the old school tie connection. This association is particularly connected with old boys from Eton and Harrow schools, and graduates of Oxford and Cambridge universities. The actual wearing of the old school tie is not always necessary to identify other members of the network as their somewhat exaggerated pronunciation of speech identifies them as belonging to this elite, known disparagingly, as 'toffs'.

Scouts are seen worldwide.

■ **LEFT:** Eton & Harrow school ties.
■ **RIGHT:** Robert Baden-Powell, founder of the Scouts.

This youth movement originated in Britain where it was founded in 1907 by Robert Baden-Powell. Its aims are to foster and support young people in their physical, mental and spiritual development so that they become useful members of society. Their traditional uniform is famous for its neckerchief, which is intended to unify all classes of society and hide any cultural differences. Scouts activities have their emphasis on outdoor and practical activities, mainly camping, woodcraft, sport and the like for which badges are worn to denote a standard has been attained in a particular activity.

The Virgin Group is instantly associated with the name Branson. (Sir) Richard Branson went into business after leaving school at 16, in 1966. After publishing *The Student* magazine, he then branched out into the music business, first selling records, then his own Virgin Records label that, in 1973, had a massive hit with Mike Oldfield's *Tubular Bells*. Branson has been quoted as saying that he chose the Virgin name because he was a virgin in business. Over the following 30 years or so his activities have expanded rapidly, launching companies like Virgin Atlantic Airlines, soft drinks, health clubs, limobikes and limousines, radio stations, trains, mobile phone operations and fibre-optic media, all bearing the Virgin name. More

Scouts:

First rally held: 1909 at Crystal Palace, London, attended by 10,000 boys.

Membership: Over 31 million (2008) in 216 countries.

recently, he has entered the world of space flights for paying customers, while banking has also joined the group, with the start of Virgin Money. Branson also owns Necker Island, in the Caribbean, where he

The Old School Tie:

Old Etonians: Princes William and Harry; Nineteen British Prime Ministers, including Gladstone, Walpole and David Cameron.

Old Harrovians: Winston Churchill, Robert Peel, Jawaharlal Nehru, King Hussein of Jordan, horseracing celebrity John McCririck, singer James Blunt and actor Benedict Cumberbatch.

and the chosen few can holiday in private luxury surroundings.

Many of the companies bearing the Virgin brand are owned either wholly or in part by others, returning revenues of over £13 billion in 2012, with Branson astutely taking a share of the profits, over £3 billion, from over 400 individual Virgin-branded ventures, much of the income resulting from licensing the Virgin brand. Branson claims to be an entrepreneur rather than a businessman, and doesn't actually sit on the board of any of the companies within the Virgin group.

■ **ABOVE:** One of the many successful Virgin Group branded companies.

■ **LEFT:** Some of the new achievement badges launched by The Scout Association which include a 'PR' badge and a 'Street Sports' badge.

Virgin Group:

Unsuccessful business ventures: Selling Christmas trees and Budgerigars in 1966.

Records: Sold records by mail order in 1970, opened first record shop in Oxford Street in 1971.

Record label: Started in 1973; artistes include Mike Oldfield, Genesis, the Sex Pistols and the Rolling Stones.

Airlines: Set up Virgin Atlantic Airways and Virgin Cargo in 1984 using a leased Boeing 747. Fleet now (2012) comprises 38 aircraft, with orders for 28 more and options on a further 14.

Meccano, Scalextric and the Flushing Toilet

Meccano is a model construction system, comprising perforated metal plates and strips, wheels, axles and brackets that are held together with nuts and bolts. These can be used, together with winding handles, drive bells and electric motors to make working models similar to real-life items. Invented by Frank Hornby in England in 1901, and originally called 'Mechanics Made Easy', the name Meccano was adopted in 1907. Manufactured in England until 1980, it is now made in France and China. For small boys, (and their dads!), these practical kits

of parts helped realise the dreams of those who aspired to be an engineer, whether they used the included handbook for guidance or otherwise let their creative imaginations flow.

Scalextric is a well-known British brand of electric slot-racing set that was designed by Freddie Francis of Minimodels. Currently owned by Hornby, the sets were derived from a clockwork-powered, metal racing car system of the early 1950s. The name was a compound of the trade name Scalex and 'electric' and first appeared at

the Harrogate Toy Fair in 1957. Within a year, ownership transferred to Triang whose subsidiary, Rovex, then converted the originally tin-plate cars to plastic, which was easier and cheaper to produce. Later, the rubber track was also changed to plastic. With a full range of cars and track, and with many trackside accessories, Scalextric has proved a popular and absorbing hobby for kids of all ages.

Meccano:

Location: Factory and headquarters built at Binns Road, Liverpool, in 1914.

Early sets: Meccano Outfits Nos 1 to 6 were made from flimsy, crudely made steel plate. In 1922, the No 7 Outfit was made from sturdier steel with rounded edges; wheels and gears were made from brass.

Coloured pieces: Introduced for 25th anniversary in 1926, when red and green pieces became 'Meccano in Colours'.

Owners: Triang (Lines Bros), 1964; Airfix Industries, 1972; sold to US-based General Mills in 1981, when production moved to France.

■ **BELOW: Titanic model made by a Meccano enthusiast, on display at the TITANICA exhibition at the Transport Museum in Belfast.**

Scalextric:

First model cars: 1957 – Metal-bodied Ferrari 375 and Maserati 250F, with a gimballed, electric pick-up.

First with headlights: 1962 – Lister Jaguar and Aston Martin DBR.

Digital controllers introduced: 2004.

James Bond set: Introduced in 1967, featuring the Mercedes 190 SL Sports and Bond's famous Aston Martin DB5 with working ejector seat and car flipper at the rear. Originally costing £11, a James Bond set fetched £1,300 in an auction held in 2005.

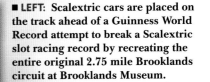

■ **LEFT:** Scalextric cars are placed on the track ahead of a Guinness World Record attempt to break a Scalextric slot racing record by recreating the entire original 2.75 mile Brooklands circuit at Brooklands Museum.

■ **BELOW:** Thomas Crapper, inventor of the flushing toilet.

The Flushing Toilet is not a modern invention. In its crudest, modern form it dates back to 1596, when a flushing toilet was invented by John Harrington. A flushing 'water closet' was patented by Yorkshireman Joseph Bramah in 1778. However, much of the credit for the modern flushing toilet is given to Thomas Crapper, a plumber and sanitary engineer, although the original patent for this convenient device was awarded to Albert Giblin in 1898. Thomas Crapper, whose surname has become a popular euphemism for the toilet, came to the fore after being awarded a Royal Warrant in the 1880s by Prince Edward (later, King Edward VII), for the supply of 30 lavatories and enclosures for Sandringham House, Norfolk. This seal of approval led to further Royal Warrants and helped to establish Crapper, along with Thomas Twyford the pottery maker, in the forefront of British sanitary engineering.

Flushing Toilet:

First recorded instance: *circa* 31st century BC in Britain's oldest Neolithic village, Skara Brae, Orkney, which used river water to flush waste away.

Types of flushing mechanism: Valveless, plunger/syphonic system (common in UK); flap valve (Europe and USA).

Curiosities: High-level, chain-operated flush was used to increase water pressure. Crapper also made manhole covers; examples may be seen within Westminster Abbey.

Cricket

Cricket was first played in southern England in the 16th century, although it may have been played as early as the 13th century. By the end of the 18th century, it had developed into the national sport, played in summer on many village greens, club and county grounds, and test match venues. The game has spread around the world, mainly in former British colonial territories, and is played at international level between teams representing nations such as Australia, New Zealand, India, Pakistan, South Africa, Sri Lanka and various countries of the Caribbean area that unite to play under the West Indies banner.

The essence of the game of cricket is that of fair play, otherwise known as 'The Spirit of the Game'. Notwithstanding the written rules of the game, it is played in a gentlemanly manner, generally known as 'playing cricket' or 'playing the game'. This includes the sportsmanlike behaviour exhibited when a player 'walks' or voluntarily gives up his wicket, or declines to claim a 'catch', even though the umpires may have given a decision to the opposite effect. Terms from the game have found

RÉPUBLIQUE FRANÇAISE

Ministère du Commerce, de l'Industrie, des Postes et des Télégraphes

EXPOSITION UNIVERSELLE DE 1900

Direction Générale de l'Exploitation

MATCH DE CRICKET
FRANCE
CONTRE
ANGLETERRE

DIMANCHE 19 ET LUNDI 20 AOUT

De 11 heures du Matin à 6 heures du Soir

AU

Vélodrome de Vincennes

TRIBUNES, 1 FRANC. — SECONDES, 50 CENTIMES

Vu : le Commissaire Général de l'Exposition Universelle de 1900

A. PICARD

■ BELOW: Sussex playing Kent at Brighton in 1849.

24

their way into the vocabularies of many English-speaking nations. Expressions such as, 'that's not cricket' (unfair), 'had a good innings', 'sticky wicket' and 'bowled over, are commonplace.

The complex rules of cricket have been summarised, as follows: 'You have two sides, one out in the field and one in. Each man that's in the side that's in goes out, and when he's out he comes in and the next man goes in until he's out. When they are all out, the side that's out comes in and the side that's been in goes out and tries to get those coming in, out. Sometimes you get men still in and not out. When a man goes out to go in, the men who are out try to get him out, and when he is out he goes in and the next man in goes out and goes in. There are two men called umpires who stay out all the time and they decide when the men who are in are out. When both sides have been in and all the men are out, and both sides have been out twice after all the men have been in, including those who are not out, that is the end of the game!'

Cricket:

Milestones: Under-arm bowling was replaced by 'round arm', then 'over arm' during the 1800s; W G Grace made his debut in 1865.

Touring matches: First England tour – 1859 to North America; first Australian tour to England (by Aboriginals) – 1868.

Ashes: Series between England and Australia began in 1882.

Limited overs: First county game – 1963; first international 1971.

The Cat's Eye and the Highway Code

The Cat's Eye is a British invention that has contributed to road safety all over the world. Percy Shaw, a Yorkshireman, came up with the idea after the removal of tramlines in a local area. Shaw realised that he had used the shiny tram tracks to help him navigate the streets in the dark. Inspired by the eyes of cats shining in the dark when caught in a beam of light, Shaw applied for his patent in 1934, with the trademark Catseye being registered by his company, Reflecting Roadstuds Limited, which was founded in 1935. The lenses had been invented in the late 1920s by Richard Murray of Hertfordshire.

Traditional cats eyes consist of two pairs of reflecting glass spherical lenses set into opposing sides of a deformable rubber carrier, all set into a cast iron housing. Placed in the centre of the road, these provided guidance to motorists travelling in either direction. Resistant to damage by vehicles passing over them, the lenses were also self-cleaned by traffic forcing the rubber downwards, where a rubber seal wiped any dirt from the lens.

Highway Code is the officially recognised guide for road users in Britain. It is a requirement for all riders and drivers to be aware of its contents and instructions for safe travel on the roads. First published in April 1931, over one million copies of the book are sold every year, the majority being purchased by learner drivers preparing for their driving test. The Highway Code contains over 300 numbered rules and nine annexes, covering pedestrians, animals, cyclists and motor vehicle users, together with graphics showing road and vehicle signs, road markings and

Cat's Eye:

Red: Placed along the hard shoulder of motorways and dual carriageways, and the nearside (left) edge of major roads.

Amber: Placed on the edge of a central reservation or median.

Green: Denote slip roads at junctions.

Yellow/green: Temporary reflectors to denote lane dividers during road works.

■ **ABOVE: A copy of the Highway Code, essential reading for learner drivers.**

other safety information. Guidance on licensing requirements, documentation, penalties for road traffic offences etc. are covered within the annexes.

Many of the rules within the code are legal requirements: these are prefaced with the terms 'MUST/MUST NOT'. Advisory wordings 'should/should not' or 'do/do not', in lower case font, are *not* legal requirements but could be used in court proceedings to establish liability.

Highway Code:

Northern Ireland: Has its own version – The Official Highway Code for Northern Ireland.

Scotland and Wales: Bi-lingual signs are not covered by the Highway Code but this code applies to both countries.

Cost: First edition was one penny in 1931; current version (2012) is £2.50.

easyJet and Dyson

easyJet is the second-largest low-cost airline in Europe. With headquarters at Luton, it has expanded rapidly since it was founded in 1995 by (now, Sir) Stelios Haji-Ioannou. Its popularity is largely due to a pricing structure that brought air travel to millions of passengers at an affordable cost. With direct booking, either by phone or Internet, the airline has effectively cut out the middleman from the booking process, helping to keep the costs low. With its largest hub at Gatwick, the airline's fleet has expanded from two leased aircraft at start-up to over 200, all Airbuses, in 2012. With 19 bases in Europe, and carrying over 42 million passengers in 2010, its route network has expanded from the original two destinations, to Edinburgh and Glasgow from London Luton, and now covers places as far apart as Scandinavia, Turkey, Egypt and the Canary Islands. The easyJet phenomenon has lived up to the advertising slogans painted on its orange and white-painted aircraft, 'Come on, let's fly' and 'The Web's Favourite Airline'.

Dyson is a name that is instantly associated with the cyclonic, bagless vacuum cleaner, found in the households of many British people and worldwide. Its founder, (Sir) James Dyson, created the first of his

■ **ABOVE:** Sir Stelios Haji-Ioannou – founder of easyJet.

■ **BELOW:** The Luton-based group, which operates more than 580 routes across 30 countries.

easyJet:

Aircraft: All from the Airbus family. A319 (156 seats) – the world's largest operator – and A320 (180 seats).

British hubs: Largest four are Gatwick, Luton, Stansted, Bristol.

Average fleet age: 3.6 years (October 2010).

radical designs with the Ballbarrow in 1974, with a ball replacing the conventional wheel. Inspired by the extraction system in the paint shop of his Ballbarrow factory, Dyson came up with the idea of applying the principle of 'cyclonic separation' to a vacuum cleaner that would not lose suction while picking up dirt. After failing to convince major manufacturers to take up the idea, he founded his own design centre and factory at Malmesbury, Wiltshire in 1993. Other Dyson innovations include the Airblade hand-drier, the blade-less Air Multiplier fan, the Dyson Hot room heater and the Dyson Ball vacuum cleaner range. In 2002, The James Dyson Foundation was endowed to encourage and support education in British design and engineering.

■ **RIGHT:** Sir James Dyson presents the vacuum cleaner models DC 02 and DC 03 in 1998.

■ **BELOW:** The versatility of a Dyson built for smaller abodes.

Dyson:

Honours and Awards: Prince Philip Designers Prize, 1997; Appointed Knight Batchelor (KB), 2007.

Personal wealth: Estimated at £1.1 billion (*Sunday Times Rich List*, 2007).

Properties owned: Dodington Park, Gloucestershire; a chateau in France; a town house in Chelsea, London.

Fish & Chips and Ice Cream Vans

Eaten with salt and vinegar, from a paper wrapping, fish & chips is one of the great British institutions. After almost 150 years, the dish has remained a firm favourite and is the top-selling fast food, despite the invasion of the burger from the USA. Mentioned in 1839 by Charles Dickens in *Oliver Twist*, fried fish is popular with British people of all generations, especially the working population. Originally

■ **ABOVE: A traditional British 'Chippie'.**

Fish & Chips:

Chips: Traditional British chips have a smaller surface area per unit weight than French fries and thus absorb less oil per weight of potato.

Batter: Usually a simple flour and water recipe, sometimes sodium bicarbonate or beer is added for lightness.

Fish: Cod or haddock are most popular; coley, pollock, plaice and rock salmon (huss) are common alternatives.

Usage: Fish and chip sales make up 25% of all white fish, and 10% of potatoes, consumed in Britain.

Portions: Greatest number sold in one day was over 4,000 portions from the same outlet.

Ice Cream Vans:

Makers: British company, Whitby Morrison, is the largest manufacturer in the world, exporting to over 60 countries.

Bodywork: Usually custom-built fibreglass or aluminium on a conventional van or truck chassis.

Operators: Usually, individually owned and run. Some are franchised by larger manufacturers.

Numbers: In decline since 2005, when an estimated 20,000 existed. In 2011, this number had shrunk to around 5,000.

Legislation: Some London boroughs will only allow 15 minutes trading, per street, per day. Many local authorities ban static sales from any one street location.

sold as separate items in small businesses in industrial Britain in the 1850s, chips were popular in the North, while battered, fried fish was a staple food in the East End of London. It is believed that the railways had some part in the combination of the northern and southern favourites, with the 'chippy' or 'chipper', rapidly spreading throughout the country. Traditionally, lard was used as the deep-frying agent: more recently, healthier vegetable oils are commonplace. Since 2003, the type of fish in the dish must be named by the vendor, leading to 'cod and chips' or 'haddock and chips' being a common order.

Ice Cream Vans are a feature of the British summer, either parked at events and attractions or, in their natural habitat, the streets of housing estates. Sounding their distinctive musical chimes, such as that based on the tune *Greensleeves*, these brightly coloured vehicles dispense ice creams, ice lollies and soft drinks to their eager clients, usually children. Originally, ice cream vans carried blocks of ice to keep their products cold: later, the on-board refrigeration unit became

available. This led to development of two different styles of ice cream: 'hard' vans sold the more traditional scoop-type product, while 'soft' vans have a soft-serve, 'whippy'-style product that is often sold with a chocolate flake inserted into the ice cream cone, this being famously

known as a '99'. Fierce rivalry often exists over territories patrolled by competing vans, in extreme cases, leading to the so-called 'ice cream wars' in the 1980s.

■ **ABOVE: All the fun of the fair rounded off with an ice cream or two!**

Cuppa, Cadbury and Conkers

Cuppa is an informal British contraction of the term 'cup of...' usually meaning a cup of tea, when somebody is asked, 'Do you fancy a cuppa?'. The first known use of the term is believed to date to 1934.

Arguments exist over the correct way to make a cuppa: most people are happy for it to be 'wet and warm', others have more fastidious requirements such as milk first or milk last. Drunk from the finest bone china or large mug, the cuppa has become an integral part of the British way of life – whether it be with 'one lump or two' – the choice is a matter of personal taste.

Cadbury is a name that means one thing to British people everywhere – chocolate! John Cadbury was a grocer who started selling cocoa and drinking chocolate in the 1820s. In 1905, Cadbury

Cuppa:

Quotes: *'Love and scandal are the best sweeteners of tea'* – **Henry Fielding**.

'Tea is meant to be bitter, just as beer is meant to be bitter' – **George Orwell**.

'I'd rather have a cup of tea than go to bed with someone – any day' – **Boy George**.

A song performed by The Kinks (1971) has the line: *'Tea knows no segregation, no class nor pedigree...'.*

■ **LEFT: A 'Cuppa' helps ease the stress of a delayed flight.**

Cadbury:

Notable product milestones: Easter Eggs – 1875; Milk Chocolate – 1897; Bourneville – 1908; Flake – 1920; Creme Egg – 1923; Roses – 1938; Fudge – 1948; Dairy Milk Buttons – 1960; Picnic – 1968; Curly Wurly – 1970; Double Decker – 1976; Wispa – 1983; Time Out – 1992; Dairy Milk Bliss – 2010.

■ **ABOVE:** An early piece of Cadbury's advertising.

■ **BELOW:** October is the month when horse-chestnut trees usually produce their crop of conkers, but over the past five years it has begun earlier and earlier.

launched the Dairy Milk bar in competition with Swiss-made imports: it was so successful that it is still sold today, although the company is no longer British owned. Cadbury bought out its rival, Fry's, in 1919, becoming the largest chocolate maker in Britain: it is now the second-largest manufacturer in the world. The company also owns Maynards and Halls, famous for its Mentho-lyptus cough soothers. Other notable brands in the Cadbury range include Milk Tray, Flake, Buttons and Heroes.

Conkers is a traditional children's game played using the seeds of the horse-chestnut tree. A conker is drilled through and threaded onto a string, which is then knotted at one end. Traditionally, an old bootlace was used but any string will do. Played by two players, the object of the game is to take turns at striking the opponent's conker until one breaks, leaving the surviving conker as a 'one-er', it having defeated 'one' other conker. A player lets his conker dangle on the string while the opponent attempts to strike it with another. A winning conker takes on the previous score of any defeated conker, plus the score for that contest: hence, a 'one-er' defeating a 'two-er' becomes a 'four-er'. Hard conkers are best: this is achieved by baking, soaking in vinegar or painting with nail varnish. Competitions have banned competitors from using their own conkers in case they have been artificially hardened, this being considered as cheating, by many.

Conkers:

Regional variations: Obblyonkers, cheggies, cheesers (a conker with a flat side, being a twin or triplet from one pod), or cheggers (Lancashire, 1920s).

First recorded: Using horse chestnuts – Isle of Wight in 1848. Previously played using hazelnuts or snail shells.

World conker championship: First held at Ashton, near Oundle, Northants, in 1965.

Cheating: Michael Palin (ex-Monty Python) was disqualified from a competition in 1993 for baking his conker and soaking it in vinegar.

The BBC, Afternoon Tea and Doctor Who

The BBC is known by people all over the world and is often their only link with Britain. Founded as a private company in 1922, it became state-owned in 1927 with its motto, 'Nation shall speak peace unto Nation'. Funded by a mandatory licence fee, for listeners and viewers in the United Kingdom, its influence has spread far and wide, mainly because of BBC Radio (formerly known as 'the wireless') through its World Service, which has broadcast news and many major announcements, including the declaration of WWII. Post-war, improvements in television gave viewers the opportunity of witnessing many major events, including the Coronation of Queen Elizabeth II, and sporting events such as the Grand National and the FA Cup Final. The BBC has provided a varied output of entertainment and factual programmes ranging from *Panorama*, *Question Time* and the *Nine O'clock News*, to *Dad's Army*, *Fawlty Towers* and *The Sky at Night*.

Afternoon Tea is an established and much-loved British tradition. Distinct from taking a 'cuppa', afternoon tea is a more formal affair, often taken in top-class establishments and formal tearooms. Accompanied by a selection of sandwiches, scones and cakes, the ritual is played out in formal but relaxing surroundings, where a choice of tea blends adds to the occasion. This experience does not come cheaply: prices in the most exclusive tearooms in London can cost upwards of £25 per person, with some establishments charging over £125 for two people. The Tea Guild Awards are the most

prestigious in the world held every year since the mid-1980s; theirs is the most highly prized accolade.

Doctor Who is a British science-fiction television programme, first produced and broadcast in 1963, by the BBC. Based on the premise of a Time Lord, referred to as 'The

Doctor', the stories follow him in his travels around the universe in his time machine called the TARDIS, this being an acronym for Time And Relative Dimension(s) In Space. The TARDIS is in the form of a blue London police box from the 1960s, larger on the inside

BBC:

Decentralisation: All national and world service radio output will be concentrated at Broadcasting House, London within 5-10 years from 2012. Television broadcasting is gradually being transferred to a purpose-built Media Centre at Salford Quays, Manchester. On completion in mid-2010s, BBC Television Centre, White City, London will be sold.

Television: First started in 1932 using John Logie Baird's 30-line system. First regular broadcasts by the BBC Television Service began in 1934. Moved to Alexandra Palace in 1936.

■ ABOVE: The BBC's own civil engineer, M T Tudsbery and the architect George Myers designed the Broadcasting Building which opened in 1932.

Afternoon Tea:

Best in Britain: Bettys Café Tea Rooms, Northallerton, Yorkshire has been named as the best place in Britain to enjoy afternoon tea, after gaining the Tea Guild's highest award for Top Tea Place 2012. Costs are around £29.95 per person.

The Ritz: Afternoon tea at The Ritz, London offers an extensive selection of 17 different types of loose leaf tea together with freshly-cut sandwiches with smoked salmon, cucumber, egg mayonnaise, roast ham and Cheddar cheese fillings at a cost of £42 per person.

The Atheneum, London: Holds the Tea Guild's 2012 award for Top Afternoon Tea, London.

than out. With a succession of companions and 'assistants', The Doctor travels the universe to help peoples and civilisations against a variety of foes, including the Daleks and the Cybermen. There have been 11 incarnations of The Doctor, the first being William Hartnell, and more than 35 companions, including Elisabeth Sladen and William Russell.

■ **RIGHT:** *Doctor Who* **actor Tom Baker poses with his fictional enemy, the Daleks, circa 1975.**

Doctor Who:

Also played by: (in order) Patrick Troughton, Jon Pertwee, Tom Baker, Peter Davison, Colin Baker, Sylvester McCoy, Paul McGann, Christopher Ecclestone, David Tennant and Matt Smith.

Time Lord: As a Time Lord, The Doctor has the ability to regenerate his body when near death. This allowed the series to continue when William Hartnell left the series in 1966, and has become a feature of the story whenever the lead actor is changed.

Foes: Autons and Daleks (Series 1); Cybermen (S2); Macra and the Master (S3); Davros (S4); and others such as Ice Warriors, Ogrons, Silurians and Black Guardians.

Associate character: Brigadier Lethbridge-Stewart, played by Nicholas Courtney has appeared with every Doctor except for that played by Colin Baker.

Spin-off series: *The Sarah Jane Adventures* in 2007 starred Elisabeth Sladen, a former companion of the Doctor; *Torchwood* in 2006, starring John Barrowman and Eve Myles.

Cockney Rhyming Slang and The Flying Scotsman

Cockney Rhyming Slang is a particularly odd form of linguistics, commonly used in the East End of London. It involves the replacement of a common word with a rhyming phrase of two or three words; the rhyming word is then omitted, leaving an apparently unconnected substitute as the subject. Typically the word 'stairs' becomes 'pears', from the rhyming phrase 'apples and pairs'. Believed to date from the 1840s, it was either a game, used by traders to confuse non-locals, or possibly by criminals to confuse the police.

Rhyming slang has been absorbed into everyday English language and developed to embrace modern life. Sometimes quite obscure, as in the use of 'Aris' instead of 'buttocks'; this being 'double-rhyming' slang where 'bottle and glass' – for 'ass' – is truncated to 'bottle', then *double-rhymed* with 'Aristotle Onassis' (the late Greek shipping magnate), whose first name is then shortened to 'Aris'. Double-rhyming slang is frequently used in modern urban language, with new expressions being heard almost daily. Much of this is due to the use of street language in today's television, media and entertainment, and is sometimes referred to as 'mockney'.

■ **ABOVE:** A Pearly King and Queen in their traditional outfits, on display as they pass the Mansion House in the City of London, during the annual Lord Mayor's show.

■ **BELOW:** The 'Apple and Pears' are commonly known elsewhere as 'the stairs'.

Cockney Rhyming Slang:

Cockney: 'Have a butchers' (Butchers hook) – look; 'Trouble and strife' – wife; 'Barnet' (Barnet Fair) – hair.

Modern cockney slang: 'Ruby' (Ruby Murray) – curry.

Mockney: 'Adrian' (Adrian Mole) – dole; 'Ayrton Senna' – tenner (£10 note); 'Nuclear sub' – pub (from the film *Lock, Stock and Two Smoking Barrels*).

The Flying Scotsman is probably the best-known railway train in Britain. This express train runs between London and Edinburgh on the East Coast rail network. First run in 1862, with simultaneous departures from London King's Cross and Edinburgh Waverley at 10:00, the journey took 10½ hours including a half-hour stopover at York for lunch. By 1888, the journey time had reduced to 8½ hours. Since 1900, the advent of connected corridor coaches and dining cars increased passengers' comfort, although there was still a short stopover in York. From 1928, new locomotives with corridor tenders, for crew changes, allowed the services to become non-stop. The famous A1 Pacific-class locomotive, No 4472, *Flying* *Scotsman,* hauled the inaugural service from London on 1 May 1928: this famous engine, beloved by steam enthusiasts, is preserved in the National Railway Museum, York. The *Flying Scotsman* name is still used by the private operators of Anglo-Scottish trains on the East Coast main line.

Flying Scotsman:

Speed: *Flying Scotsman,* No 4472, was the first locomotive to officially exceed 100mph (62kph) in 1934.

Distance record: In 1988-89 during a tour of Australia, *Flying Scotsman* No 4472 recorded the longest-ever, non-stop run by a steam locomotive, travelling 422 miles (679 km).

Previous owners: Alan Pegler (1960s) bought No 4472 from British Rail for £3,000; Record producer Pete Waterman was a part-owner in the 1990s.

■ **RIGHT:** *The Flying Scotsman* **in the restoration workshops of the National Railway Museum, 2010.**

Full English Breakfast and HP Sauce

A Full English Breakfast is a substantial meal consisting of several courses. This includes a starter of fruit juice, fresh fruit or cereal, a fried main course, followed by toast and marmalade, accompanied by a hot beverage such as tea or coffee. In more recent times, the main course alone has become known as the 'full English' or a 'fry-up'. Regional variations include the 'full Scottish', 'full Irish', 'full Welsh', or the 'Ulster fry'. The full English usually contains fried bacon, sausage, fried bread, fried egg, mushrooms and/ or tomato. The regional variations often include, black or white pudding, corned-beef hash, fried potato, bubble-and-squeak and fried local bread products. Traditionally, brown sauce, tomato ketchup or, sometimes, English mustard accompany the meal. Much loved by manual workers such as builders and truck drivers, with around 850 calories in the fry-up alone, the 'full English' has become an established part of British life.

HP Sauce is enjoyed by many British people, especially those partial to a bacon sandwich, and ex-pats around the world. Invented by a grocer from Nottingham, Frederick Garton, the name was registered in 1895. Garton named

■ **ABOVE INSET: Black pudding is a traditional accompaniment to a 'full English' in some parts of Britain.**

38

the sauce 'HP' after hearing that it was being served in a restaurant in the Houses of Parliament, a picture of which has appeared on the label for many years. Garton sold the recipe and brand name to Edwin Moore, founder of the Midlands Vinegar Company (later HP Foods) for £150, and it was launched commercially in 1905. Ingredients include tomatoes, malt vinegar, molasses, glucose-fructose syrup, spirit vinegar, sugar, dates, corn flour, rye flour, salt, spices, flavourings and tamarind. Users protested over the substitution of much of the salt content by a reduced-sodium alternative, following government directives over salt content in foods. In the 1960s and 70s, HP Sauce became known as Wilson's gravy, after the PM's known habit of pouring it over most of his food.

HP Sauce:

Inventor claims: It has been alleged that Harry Palmer, a gambler, passed on the original recipe for 'Harry Palmer's Famous Epsom Salts' to Frederick Garton in settlement of a debt.

Bilingual label: For many years, the label wording appeared in both English and French. In a 1960s BBC radio broadcast, the comedian Marty Feldman sang the French words in the style of Jacques Brel; it was a track on Feldman's album, *I Feel a Song Going Off.*

British Bobby and Marks & Spencer

The British Bobby is an iconic sight on the streets of Britain, and is instantly recognised by visitors from overseas. Named after Sir Robert (Bobby) Peel, a 19th-century prime minister, and sometimes called 'a Peel-er', the bobby is the archetypal British policeman. Although the uniform has changed over the years, most people think of the pointed, dome-shaped 'custodian' helmet as being the one item of uniform that distinguishes the British bobby from most other police forces around the world. Seen in several variations including the 'crested' type, the helmet has been replaced by the flat, peaked cap in most police forces, although they may still be seen on the streets, especially in London. The 'bobby on the beat' historically patrolled alone and, if assistance was needed, would blow his whistle to attract attention. Sadly, due to reductions in manpower, this is no longer the case: instead, patrols are often carried out in motor vehicles. The bobby on his bike, once a familiar sight in most neighbourhoods, is now a rarity, unless mounted on a modern all-terrain bicycle, around

British Bobby:

Custodian helmets: Made by only four manufacturers (2012) – Hobson and Sons (London) Ltd; Christys', of Stockport; Compton Webb (C W Headdress Limited), of Oxfordshire; and Helmets Limited, of Wheathampstead.

History: The custodian helmet was adopted by the Metropolitan Police in 1863 to replace the 'top-hat' style headgear.

pedestrianised city centres.

Marks & Spencer is a classic British brand. With over 700 stores in the UK, and a further 300 in 40 countries worldwide, 'Marx & Sparks', sometimes 'M&S' or simply 'Marks', is a name that is widely respected for selling quality clothing, homeware and luxury food products. Michael Marks started from humble beginnings in 1884, with a market stall in Leeds, and had opened market stalls all over the north-west of England by the time he entered business with Thomas Spencer: they opened their first store in Manchester in 1894. This was the beginning of an empire that became a giant in British retailing. In 1998, it was the first British retailer to make a pre-tax profit of over £1 billion. With a policy (until 2002) of selling only British-made goods, M&S became famous

■ **LEFT:** The beginnings of Marks & Spencer. Michael Marks, left and Thomas Spencer, 1900.

for its generous returns policy, insisting 'The customer *is always and completely right*'. Its famous

St Michael brand has been around since 1928 although, until around 1950, ladies and girls clothing was sold under the *St Margaret* label. After a difficult trading period, this stock-market listed company is, once again, thriving and remains a favourite with shoppers around the world.

Marks & Spencer:

Plastic bags: Marks & Spencer became one of the first retailers to charge for plastic carrier bags to encourage use of multi-trip alternatives.

Plan A: M&S launched this initiative in 2007, with the aim of becoming 'carbon neutral' within five years.

Energy: Three wind turbines are operated on behalf of M&S, which provide sufficient energy for the National Grid to power three of its stores.

Carry On Films

Carry On Films are a popular form of cinema entertainment dating from 1958. This low-budget series was made at a time when British social values were much different from those of today. The films poked fun at the establishment and were, often, shamelessly sexist. Featuring scantily-clad females, and with male characterisations that were either extremely coarse or highly camp, the scripts were littered with innuendo and '*double-entendres*'. The series featured 29 original films and one compilation, made between 1958 and 1978 at Pinewood Studios: early releases were made in black-and-white. The last, *Carry On Columbus,* was made in 1992 and featured only a few of the actors from the earlier productions. Produced by Peter Rogers and directed by Gerald Thomas, screenplays were written by comedy writers of the calibre of Norman Hudis and Talbot Rothwell. Featuring a regular cast, the most-seen actor of the series was Kenneth Williams, who appeared in 26, with Joan Sims (24) Charles Hawtrey, (23) and Sid James (19).

   Parodies of serious films such as *Carry On Cleo,* in 1964, added to the range of titles that first began in 1958 with *Carry On Sergeant,* starring William Hartnell, Bob Monkhouse and Eric Barker. The budget for this film was around £74,000, small by today's standards, yet it grossed over £500,000 at British box offices alone. The final film from the original series, *Carry On Emmanuelle*, with Kenneth Williams, Kenneth Connor, Joan Sims and Suzanne Danielle was made on a budget of £320,000. No section of British life was immune from the Carry On treatment: hospitals (*Carry On Nurse*), schools

Carry On Films:

Largest UK audience: *Carry On Nurse* was seen by 10.4 million and was the highest-grossing film of 1959. Also successful in the USA, it played in cinemas there for three years.

Stage shows: *Carry On London* (1973-75) Victoria Palace; *Carry On Laughing* (1976), Royal Opera House, Scarborough; *Wot A Carry On In Blackpool* (1992) was a revue starring Barbara Windsor and Bernard Bresslaw.

Television documentary: *What's A Carry On* was a 50-minute programme in 1998 to celebrate the 40th anniversary of the first film.

■ **ABOVE:** Actress Fenella Fielding, who played Valeria in *Carry On Screaming*, launches the Royal Mail's new stamp series celebrating the 50th anniversary of the *Carry On* series of films and of the first *Dracula* movie by Hammer Films, 2008.

■ **LEFT:** Sid James (seated) as Henry VIII and Terry Scott as Cardinal Wolsey in *Carry On Henry*.

■ **RIGHT:** *Carry On* legend Barbara Windsor.

(*Teacher*), police (*Constable*), hospitals again, twice (*Carry On Doctor* and *Carry On Again, Doctor*). Barbara Windsor made her series début, the first of 10 appearances, in 1964 in *Carry On Spying*. Only two of the series does not have the words 'Carry On' in the title: *Don't Lose Your Head* (1966) and *Follow That Camel* (1967), although the latter was prefixed with *Carry On* – to become *Carry On, Follow That Camel*, outside the UK. Often seen nowadays on television, the 'Carry On' series was a watershed in Britain's comedy film heritage.

Television:

John Logie Baird (1888-1946): By the time he was 12 years old, Baird had developed a four-way telephone exchange system and installed electric lighting in his parents' house powered by a petrol-engined generator in the back garden.

Education: Slow and timid at school, Baird took an eight-year diploma course in electrical engineering followed by a BSc degree at Glasgow University.

■ **BELOW:** John Logie Baird, engineer and inventor of the television, was married to Margaret Cecilia Albu, British concert pianist, at the Half Moon Hotel in Coney Island, New York, 1931.

Television and Coronation Street

Television is largely due to the work of John Logie Baird, a Scottish inventor who first demonstrated the principle in London's Soho in 1925. Baird's process utilised a Nipkow disc, operating at a mechanical 30-lines scan, to transmit moving silhouette images. By 1926, he had transmitted a barely-discernible human face, that of office boy William Taynton, who was paid two shillings and sixpence (12½ pence) for that honour. The following year, Baird invented 'Phonovision', a system of recording television images onto a 10-inch (25.4cm) wax audio disc. After developing an improved photoelectric

cell, and improving the picture using his electronic 'sharpening' method, Baird was able to produce a viable television picture, which formed the basis of true television as we know it today. His genius was then applied to development of workable forms of colour and three-dimensional television, and radar technology devices.

Coronation Street is loved by many

television viewers, both in Britain and around the world. Set in the fictional town of Weatherfield in Greater Manchester, the story documents the lives of working-class people. First broadcast on ITV's Granada Television on 9 December 1960, the programme has run continuously since then, becoming the world's longest-running TV soap opera: this belies the statement written by *Daily Mirror* columnist, Ken Irwin, who probably regretted his forecast that it would only last three weeks.

'The Street', as it became known, was responsible for bringing the northern-English dialect into popular culture. Sayings like 'By heck!', 'all right, chook?', 'nowt' and 'owt' were heard outside of their usual habitat for the first time: some viewers around the country struggled with this vernacular. The main characters have endured:

■ **ABOVE:** Peter Adamson, as Len Fairclough, Philip Lowrie as Dennis Tanner and Graham Haberfield as Jerry Booth in *Coronation Street*, 1966.

Ken Barlow (played by William Roache) was the only original member of the cast until 2011, when Dennis Tanner (Philip Lowrie) returned after 43 years absence. Roache is the longest-serving actor in any soap opera in the world. Early characters, such as the waspish Ena Sharples, the timid Minnie Caldwell and their cohort Martha Longhurst, would sit in the 'snug' bar of the Rovers Return pub, the focal point of the series, and pass judgement and opinions over all in the street.

Other favourite characters were Elsie Tanner, publicans Jack Walker and his snobbish wife Annie, their barmaid Betty Williams, Stan and Hilda Ogden, Bet Lynch, and Jack and Vera Duckworth. More recently, the Battersby family, Gail Platt and Sally Webster have kept the pot boiling.

■ **RIGHT:** Former *Coronation Street* star Julie Goodyear during a photocall for the *Street of Dreams*, which was a *Coronation Street* live show in Manchester.

Coronation Street:

Original scriptwriter: Tony Warren wrote the first 13 episodes and was script consultant for many years since.

Theme music: Signature tune was written by Eric Spear.

Highest viewer ratings: Christmas Day 1987 – around 28.5 million tuned in to watch as Hilda Ogden left 'The Street'.

Average viewing figures: Between 1960s and 1980s – over 20 million per episode; currently between 8 and 14 million per episode.

Wide-screen: Episode 5191, on 7 January 2002, was the first to be broadcast in 16:9 wide-screen format. *Coronation Street* was the last British soap to make the switch from 4:3 format.

The Swinging Sixties and the Miniskirt

The Swinging Sixties is best remembered for the changes in social attitudes and popular culture that occurred during the 1960s, along with the stylish clothing and distinctive music of the period. This decade brought The Beatles and the Rolling Stones, Bob Dylan and Jimi Hendrix: with them came styles of dress previously unseen in Britain.

Mary Quant and Twiggy were at the forefront of fashion; fads of the time included bell-bottom trousers, Paisley-print material and tie-die fabrics. Hairstyles for men included the mop top, as favoured by The Beatles, while women's styles ranged from the bouffant, or beehive, to the Twiggy cut.

Attitudes towards sex and drugs changed significantly, particularly among younger people. Here sexual freedom, partly due to the newly available contraceptive pill, and moral laxity became relatively commonplace. Recreational drug use also became fashionable with the use of marijuana and LSD – surprisingly still legal until 1966 – while amphetamines became the driving force behind the 'dance till you drop' culture of the scooter-riding 'Mods'. Their motorcycling opponents, the 'Rockers', took on the 'Mods' in pitched battles at south coast seaside resorts during 1964, after which a judge labelled these warring factions as 'sawdust Caesars'.

On the music front, 'pirate' radio stations dropped anchor around

Swinging Sixties:

Fashion models: Jean Shrimpton, known as 'The Face of the Sixties' and models such as Veruschka, Penelope Tree and Twiggy ('The Face of 1966') symbolised the fashion revolution.

Designers: Mary Quant was the leader of '60s fashion, largely responsible for the 'mod' fashion movement. Innovations such as knickerbockers, PVC plastics and coloured tights came into fashion along with the miniskirt and 'hot pants'.

Music: Groups such as The Who, The Kinks, The Small Faces and Pink Floyd stormed onto the music scene during the '60s, becoming style icons as well as musicians.

■ **BELOW: Mary Quant, foreground, with models showing her new shoe creations.**

46

Miniskirt:

Dolly-birds: Nickname given to wearers of the miniskirt and white PVC boots.

Biba: Their Kensington shop sold miniskirts that were 10 inches (25cm) long.

Materials: Miniskirts were made from a range of materials including wool, silk, PVC, acrylics and denim.

the coasts of Britain, bringing their illegal, but highly sought after, broadcasts to eager listeners who were fed-up with the same old diet of mainly light or classical music from out-of-touch mainstream radio stations. Over 30 pirate stations, including Radio Caroline and Radio Veronica, and some other relatively short-lived broadcasters, satisfied the demand for popular music that exploded onto the sixties scene. Eventually, the BBC saw the light and launched Radio 1 in 1967. Films like *Blowup* and *Alfie* (both in 1966), and television series like *The Avengers* (1961-69) caught the mood and style of this unforgettable decade.

The Miniskirt was the most defining fashion statement of the 1960s. Popularised by Mary Quant, its development was claimed to be the work of either André Courrèges or John Bates. Since the late 1950s, skirt lengths had risen to just above the knee: this was considered a sensible trend as it allowed a more active lifestyle for wearers. Mary Quant claimed it was her customers who demanded even shorter skirts, to the point where they were called 'pelmets' by their detractors. The garment had a massive impact on wearers and watchers alike: the King's Road in London's Chelsea became a hotspot for fashion fans who tried to out-do each other as hemlines moved higher and higher. Carnaby Street also sold the 'mini' in its already extravagant, boutique-style shops.

■ **ABOVE:** The hemlines were risky in the sixties but have risen ever further in more recent times.

Sunday Roast and Colman's English Mustard

Sunday Roast is a traditional British main meal served on Sundays, usually around midday or early in the afternoon. Also known as Sunday dinner, the meal consists of a roasted joint of meat, with roasted, boiled or mashed potato, Yorkshire pudding and gravy, and, usually,

Sunday Roast:

Traditions: Dripping was used to roast the meat and Yorkshire pudding – the meat juices were then used to make the gravy, together with gravy browning or corn flour and, most importantly, an OXO cube.

Potatoes: Best roasted when placed around the meat, so they cook in the same oil or fat.

Resting time: Meat is removed from the oven and left in a warm place to rest: this is said to both enhance the flavour and make it easier to carve.

two types of vegetable. Beloved by British people, this is the must-have meal for a Sunday lunch or other special occasion. In recent times this type of meal has become popular in pubs and restaurants, where it is usually called a carvery.

The origin of the Sunday roast is believed to date back to Mediaeval times when, after Sunday morning church service, serfs would practise their battle skills; afterwards, they were rewarded by the squire with a spit-roasted ox for their midday meal. A more modern origin dates from the Industrial Revolution, when Yorkshire families left a cut of meat in the oven to roast while they went to church, the meat being ready by the time they returned home. This version is favoured by many, as it is the most likely origin of roast meat being served together with Yorkshire pudding. Whatever its origin, the Sunday roast remains a favourite of the British people and shows no sign of being displaced from its ranking as the nation's favourite meal.

Colman's English Mustard is a traditional British accompaniment to roast beef or pork, and is highly regarded as a flavour enhancer for cold meats, particularly ham. First made by Jeremiah Colman in 1814, the strongly-flavoured Colman's English Mustard (not to be confused with any wimpish French counterpart!) has graced the tables of British families ever since. Originally sold only as a powder in tins, the readymade variant in jars, tubes and sachets has brought the product up-to-date for today's consumers. The Colman's Mustard Shop, with its Victorian themed premises, is a popular tourist stop in the city of Norwich.

Colman's English Mustard:

In 1903, Colman's bought rival mustard maker Keen & Son, this is the believed origin of the expression, 'keen as mustard'.

From 1880-1939, Colman's issued special pictorial tins each year – including those in 1902 to celebrate the Coronation of Edward VII.

The bull's head first appeared on Colman's English Mustard in 1855 – as a symbol of tradition and quality.

49

Football

Football is the national sport of Britain. Otherwise known as 'soccer' (derived from Association Football) or 'footie', football has, in the last 150 years, become the most popular sport in the United Kingdom. With players of all ages, from the smallest club or village team, to the highly-paid players in the top tier of the professional game, football has become a national passion. Britain is considered to be the origin of the modern game, now played all over the world. Early ball games played by Ancient Greeks and Romans developed into more organised forms of the game by Mediaeval times, and became formalised in public schools in the early 16th century. The football, as an object, was referenced in 1486, in a poem of the day, as being: *'a certain rounde instrument to play with... it is an instrument for the foote and then it is calde in Latyn 'pila pedalis', a fotebal.'*

Richard Mulcaster, a public school's headmaster, is credited with early organisation of the sport: terms like 'sides' (teams), 'standings' (positions), 'judge over the parties' (referee), and 'trayning maister' (coach) appeared in his writings. In 1863, representatives of various football clubs in the London area met, with the aim of unifying the various rules that differed between them. On 8 December 1863, the Football Association (FA) published the 'Laws of Football' that form the basis for the game as it exists today: the FA remains the controlling body for the sport. The oldest football club in the world is Sheffield FC, founded in 1857, with their first inter-club game being played in 1860 against Hallam FC; Sheffield FC won 2-0. The oldest professional 'league' club is Notts County FC, founded in 1862: this club was one of the 12 founder members of the Football League (in 1888) and has been a member of the oldest league competition in

■ **BELOW: The FA Cup Final between Wolves & Everton, 1893.**

the world ever since. From these beginnings, the game as we know it today has developed beyond the amateur clubman's game to become a top spectator sport, attended by millions of spectators every year.

■ **ABOVE:** An engraving showing 'Football in Crowe Street', 1721.

Football:

Football banned: In 1363, King Edward III issued a proclamation banning '...handball, football, or hockey; coursing and cock-fighting, or other such idle games'.

Tudor times: A pair of football boots was ordered by King Henry VIII in 1526. Women played a form of football in 1580, as described by poet Sir Philip Sidney: 'When she, with skirts tuckt very hy, with girles at football playes'.

Early overseas tour: In 1586, men from a ship commanded by an English explorer named John Davis, went ashore to play a form of football with Inuit (Eskimo) people in Greenland.

The Mini Car and WHSmith

The Mini Car is an iconic British design that was voted the second most influential car of the 20th century, after the Model T Ford. Designed by Alec Issigonis, the classic Mini was built in various guises between 1958 and 2000. Larger than expected on the inside, the Mini featured a transverse engine and transmission: this left over 80% of the floor pan available for passengers and luggage. Initially marketed as the Austin Mini and Morris Minor, the name Mini became a marque in its own right in 1969. Loved by many during the Swinging Sixties as a style icon, the advent of the sportier Mini Cooper and Mini Cooper S models brought success in rally competitions,

■ **ABOVE: A Mini Cooper at the Motor Show, 1997.**

Mini Car:

Limited Editions: The Mini Mayfair, Mini Italian Job, Mini Park Lane were very popular, if rather expensive versions.

First-ever Mini: Registered 601 AOK, the first-ever Mini was never sold publicly. It is displayed in the Heritage Motor Centre at Gaydon, Warwickshire.

Total production: A total of 5,387,862 Minis were made: 1,581,887 were sold in Britain. Over 10,000 left-hand-drive versions were exported to the USA.

Larger marques: Wolseley Hornet (28,455 built) and Riley Elf (30,912 built) variants had a larger three-box bodyshell.

including winning the Monte Carlo Rally four times in a row between 1965-67. Made in variants such as the Mini Van, Mini Moke, Mini Traveller and Mini Clubman, this much-loved vehicle was made for almost any occasion, whether for private motoring or business use.

52

WHSmith is renowned for its chain of newspaper, book and stationery shops situated on high streets, shopping malls, railway stations and airports. Famously, it was the first-ever chain-store in the world: it is also credited with creating the world's first book cataloguing system, forerunner of the ISBN system. Dating back to 1792, the company began as a news vendor: Henry Walton Smith and his wife Anna set up his business in Little Grosvenor Street, London. On their deaths, their son William Henry Smith bought the business for £1,280, a large sum in 1812. In 1846, his only son, also William Henry Smith, later a Member of Parliament, became a partner in the W H Smith & Son company. The company expanded with the railway boom and became a major distributor of newspapers, then expanded into the travel, DIY and records markets. In 1998, the company took over the John Menzies chain, expanding into Scotland. Today, the WHSmith empire includes around 580 shops and 400 travel outlets.

WHSmith:

Overseas: WHSmith operations have included shops in Ireland, Canada, the United States, Australia and India and more recently, Denmark, with six branches.

Post Office: Many branches have opened Post Office branches, as a result of closures of local sub-post offices.

Motorways: WHSmith have shops in 50 Moto motorway service areas, Welcome Break has 33, and RoadChef 29.

Ordnance Survey Maps and the Hovercraft

Ordnance Survey Maps have been around for more than 200 years. They provide accurate, detailed and reliable information for professionals and amateurs alike. Available in a wide range of scales, each scale provides a different level of information ranging from overview to the very detailed, that are suitable for hikers, and cross-country navigation. Explorer, Route and Tour maps and Landranger series are the most commonly used maps in Britain. Although the need for paper maps is a diminishing one, due largely to sat-nav systems and GPS facilities on mobile phones, Ordnance Survey provides digital services and online mapping for websites: OS Street View is the trademark for their street-level, digital background maps that provide localised geographical information for a range of different requirements, showing building outlines, roads and rivers, and woodland areas. Particularly suited

Ordnance Survey Maps:

First map produced: 1747 – King George II commissioned a map of the Scottish Highlands – scale, 1 inch to 1,000 yards – during the Jacobite rebellion.

Ordnance Survey created: Arising from the Principal Triangulation of Great Britain (1783-1853).

Wall maps: Most popular is the wall map of the World.

National security: Until the early 1940s, dockyards, military installations and other strategic information were left blank on non-military maps.

to business applications, these digital services are frequently updated and help to keep Ordnance Survey in the forefront of mapping providers.

The modern Hovercraft, or Air Cushion Vehicle (ACV), was invented by (Sir) Christopher Cockerell. Others before him had tried the lifting-fan principle but it was Cockerell who came up with the concept of trapping the fan air within a 'skirt' around the vehicle, so that lift was generated by air pressure rather than air flow. Having successfully demonstrated his model to the British government and the military, it was promptly placed on the 'secret' list. As neither the Royal Navy nor the RAF was interested, it was then declassified: Cockerell continued working with the National Research Development Corporation (NRDC) who placed a contract with Saunders-Roe for the SRN1. Powered by a 450 hp (330.97 kW) aero engine and a fan, the SRN1 made its first hover on 11 June 1959, and crossed the English Channel on 25 July 1959. Further

development led to the car-carrying SRN4 in early 1968, which operated cross-channel services from 1968 to 2000. Hovercraft still serve with the British Army, and US military, in a variety of roles.

Hovercraft:

SRN4: Capable of carrying 254 passengers and up to 30 cars (Mark I) at a speed of 83 knots (154 km/h): cruising speed was 60 knots (111 km/h).

The Royal Dent: In 1959, the Duke of Edinburgh piloted the craft at too fast a speed, causing an unrepaired dent to remain under the bow of the SRN1.

Fastest English Channel crossing: In 22 minutes by SRN4 Mk III *Princess Anne* on 14 September 1995.

Domestic hovering: Hoover Constellation vacuum cleaner and the Flymo lawn mower both use a similar hovering system.

■ **BELOW: Sir Christopher Cockerell, the inventor of the Hovercraft, takes control for a short time in the Solent of one of the latest Hovercraft to be introduced into the armed forces, 1994.**

Sandwich:

Origin: The modern sandwich is said to have originated when John Montagu, 4th Earl of Sandwich had meat between bread brought to sustain him during lengthy gambling sessions. The bread kept his hands free of grease from the meat when playing cards.

Sandwich, Strawberries & Cream, and Rolls-Royce

The Sandwich, 'Sarnie' or 'Butty' is one of the most popular forms of take-out food in Britain. Often made at home, it has been a part of the British lunch menu for many years, usually found in the 'snap' tin of manual workers. A true sandwich consists of two slices of bread, each spread with butter, and a hot or cold filling of choice: these include cheese and cucumber, jam, bacon, and sausage. For the more genteel, egg and cress, or smoked salmon, sandwiches are served with their crusts removed – unlike the hearty 'door-stop' sarnie, traditionally made with hand-cut thick, crusty bread, rather than a ready-sliced loaf.

Strawberries & Cream is a much loved summer treat, although imported strawberries have made it available all-year-round. Traditionally associated with tennis at Wimbledon, and garden parties elsewhere, English strawberries are considered to be the best, while arguments rage over which type of cream, pouring, double, or clotted, should accompany them. The term 'strawberries and cream' is sometimes used to describe the complexion of younger, white females with a particular skin tone, as being '...good enough to eat'.

Rolls-Royce is one of the most famous brand names in the world.

This iconic British company is known for its engineering excellence in the fields of motorcars, aero engines and marine engines. The name is so highly regarded that it is often used as an adjective to describe an object of exceptional quality, as being, '...the Rolls-Royce of watches [or other]'. Founded in 1906 as a partnership between Charles Stewart Rolls and

Henry Royce, the latter having began building quality cars in 1904. His first, the Royce 10, impressed Rolls such that his dealership, C S Rolls & Co of Fulham, took all the cars Royce could make. Their first success, the R-R 40/50 hp model of motorcar of 1907, was better known as the Silver Ghost: a total of 7,874 were made and some survive today.

In WWI, R-R built aero engines, first under licence from Renault, followed by their own design, the 12-cylinder Eagle, precursor of their famous range of piston aero engines named after birds of prey. Their most famous engine, the Merlin, first flew in 1935 and went on to become perhaps the most famous

Wimbledon: Strawberries & cream cost around four times the price of that sold elsewhere.

Sandwiches: In 2011 Tesco sold packaged Strawberries and Clotted Cream Sandwiches at £1 per pack – this was largely due to a bumper crop of the fruit that year.

aero engine of WWII, powering the Spitfire, Hurricane, Lancaster and Mosquito, and was called 'The engine that won the war'. The R-R range of military jet engines included the Derwent, Avon, Viper, Pegasus, Orpheus and Olympus.

Civil airliner engines such as the Dart, Tyne, Trent, and the engine that led to the nationalisation of the company in 1971, the infamously late but ultimately successful RB-211, kept the Rolls-Royce name in the forefront of modern aviation.

Rolls-Royce:

Acquisition: In 1931 Rolls-Royce acquired the much smaller rival car maker Bentley, resulting from the 1930s depression. From soon after WWII until 2002, Bentley and Rolls-Royce cars were often identical apart from the radiator grille and minor details.

Myth: In 1933, the colour of the Rolls-Royce radiator monogram was changed from red to black because the red sometimes clashed with the coachwork colour selected by clients, and *not* as a mark of respect for the passing of Royce.

57

■ **BELOW: A mechanic makes the final adjustments to the Rolls-Royce engine to be fitted to the Avro Tudor I airliner at Avro's factory at Woodford Aerodrome in Stockport, 1946.**

James Bond

James Bond is a fictional character created by Ian Fleming. Bond is portrayed as an agent of the British Secret Intelligence Service, now known as MI6, with the code number '007', and is 'Licensed to Kill'. As a Commander in the Royal Naval Reserve, Bond was based on individuals known to Ian Fleming during his own work in Naval Intelligence during WWII. Fleming, a keen birdwatcher took the name from an American ornithologist he had met, citing it was a simple, dull-sounding name. His first Bond novel, *Casino Royale*, was started in February 1952 and written at Fleming's Goldeneye estate. Here he wrote all of his 12 novels and two short stories featuring the 007 character, writing them always during the months of January and February. Initially rejected by publishers Jonathan Cape, they were subsequently (in 1953) published by them (as were all of his Bond books) on the recommendation of Fleming's brother Peter, a successful travel writer.

Even those who have never read a book will probably have heard of James Bond through the medium of film: since 1962 there have been 22 films released by Eon Productions, made usually at Pinewood Studios and exotic locations around the world. Produced by Albert R Broccoli and Harry Saltzman until 1975, then Saltzman alone until 1992, the James Bond series is the second-highest grossing film series of all time – after *Harry Potter*. First played by Sean Connery, the role of James Bond has also been played by Roger Moore, George Lazenby, Timothy Dalton, Pierce Brosnan and Daniel Craig. Featuring characters by the name of Q, Miss Moneypenny, M, and arch-villains Auric Goldfinger, Emilio Largo, Dr No and Blofeld, the James Bond character, and his famous Aston Martin DB5, is one of Britain's most famous film exports.

■ **ABOVE:** Honor Blackman (Pussy Galore) meets Sean Connery (James Bond) before the filming of the third Bond movie *Goldfinger*, 1964.

■ **BELOW:** Daniel Craig will star in *Skyfall* the much anticipated new 'Bond'.

James Bond:

Famous dialogue excerpt (from Bond films): BOND: 'Do you expect me to talk?' GOLDFINGER: 'No, Mr Bond, I expect you to die!'

Other Bond writers: Since Ian Fleming's death in 1964, six writers have written Bond books: Kingsley Amis, Christopher Wood, John Gardner, Raymond Benson, Sebastian Faulks and Jeffery Deaver. William Boyd is currently working on another, due for publication in 2013.

Radar and the Spitfire

Radar as we know it today was the invention of Sir Robert Watson-Watt who patented and demonstrated the principle of detection of aircraft, using reflected radio waves, around 1934. Although the basic concept of **Ra**dio **D**etection **a**nd **R**anging (RADAR) had been discovered in 1886, Watson-Watt's system was the first to be used as a means of defence against air attack, by detecting incoming enemy aircraft and predicting their path, and formed the basis of Britain's 'Chain Home' system in WWII. Radar is now almost universal, being used in such diverse applications as air traffic control, air defence and airborne surveillance, weather forecasting, maritime control and radar speed detection guns.

The Spitfire is perhaps the most famous fighter aircraft of WWII. Its elegant and distinctive lines belie its capability as a single-seat fighter. The sound of its Merlin, and later, Griffon,

Radar:

First principles: In 1886 Heinrich Hertz demonstrated radio reflection from static objects. Fellow German Christian Hülsmeyer detected a ship in fog, but not its distance. Hülsmeyer was granted a British patent in 1904 for his 'Telemobiloscope'.

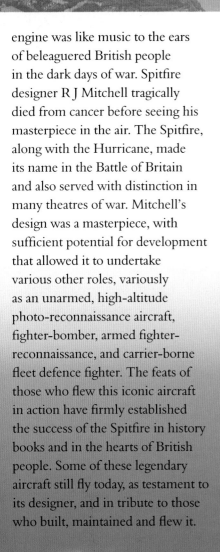

engine was like music to the ears of beleaguered British people in the dark days of war. Spitfire designer R J Mitchell tragically died from cancer before seeing his masterpiece in the air. The Spitfire, along with the Hurricane, made its name in the Battle of Britain and also served with distinction in many theatres of war. Mitchell's design was a masterpiece, with sufficient potential for development that allowed it to undertake various other roles, variously as an unarmed, high-altitude photo-reconnaissance aircraft, fighter-bomber, armed fighter-reconnaissance, and carrier-borne fleet defence fighter. The feats of those who flew this iconic aircraft in action have firmly established the success of the Spitfire in history books and in the hearts of British people. Some of these legendary aircraft still fly today, as testament to its designer, and in tribute to those who built, maintained and flew it.

■ **ABOVE: The Supermarine Spitfire British Fighters of the Fleet Air Arm peel off for a practise attack during training, 1940.**

Spitfire:

First flight: Spitfire prototype K5054 first took off on 5 March 1936, piloted by Captain Joseph 'Mutt' Summers, from Eastleigh Aerodrome, Southampton. The flight lasted for eight minutes.

Production: Largest number of any aircraft built in Britain: 20,341 Spitfires were built in 22 different variants – not including the naval Seafire.

Survivors: About 45-50 still survive (or have been rebuilt) in a flyable condition, worldwide. The oldest flyable Spitfire, a Mark IIa, P7350, of the RAF's Battle of Britain Memorial Flight actually flew in the Battle of Britain.

The Royal Family

The Royal Family, with HM Queen Elizabeth II as its head, is one of Britain's best-loved institutions. A member of the Royal Family is either born, or has married, into the House of Windsor, a dynasty that has existed since 1917. Formerly the House of Saxe-Coburg-Gotha, the name was changed to Windsor by King George V in order to distance the family name from their pre-WWI German ancestry. Prior to that year, British royal families had no surname at all, but used that of the Royal House to which they belonged. Nowadays, the surname Windsor, or Mountbatten-Windsor for direct descendants of the Queen and Prince Philip, is used on occasions when a surname is required for legal purposes. Royal princes and princesses, whose rank is prefixed 'HRH', do not legally require a surname.

Most people associate the Royal Family with great occasions of state, royal tours and visits, and other occasions where a formal and high-level British presence is needed. The Queen herself has had a busy schedule of engagements throughout her reign: even in her eighties, engagements such as ministerial audiences, investitures, home and overseas visits, and official ceremonies, such as the State Opening of Parliament, are testament to her dedication to the role as Queen of Great Britain and Northern Ireland and Head of the Commonwealth. Celebrating her Diamond Jubilee in 2012, her loyal subjects and well-wishers followed the paths of millions before them, as they gathered at events held in honour of the second-longest reigning British monarch after Queen Victoria, who reigned for 63 years and 216 days.

Some of the most unforgettable moments in recent British history have involved the Royal Family. From the Coronation of Queen Elizabeth II herself, through a number of Royal Weddings, to the Diamond Jubilee celebrations, each occasion has brought excitement, colour, and pageantry into the lives of ordinary people, whether attending the events, or seeing them on film, television, or through other forms of media. The sight of many thousands thronging the route of a royal procession along The Mall, as the Royal Family return to Buckingham Palace, is a magical event. A traditional part of all royal occasions in London is the eagerly awaited appearance of the Royal Family on the balcony of Buckingham Palace, often with a spectacular flypast adding to the occasion, as the people of Britain pay tribute to their own, very special, Royal Family.

■ **RIGHT: Queen Elizabeth II and the Duke of Edinburgh at her Coronation which took place in Westminster Abbey.**

The Royal Family:

Oldest reigning British monarch: On her 85th birthday, in 2011, Queen Elizabeth II became the oldest reigning monarch in the history of the Crown.

Family: HM the Queen and Prince Philip have four children, eight grandchildren and two great-grandchildren (as at April 2012).

Religion: HM the Queen is the Supreme Governor of the Church of England.

■ ABOVE: The Queen and Prince Albert on their return from the sacred ceremony, on 10 February 1840 The ceremony was held at St James' Palace.

■ BELOW: Queen Elizabeth II in her Jubilee Year.

The Union Flag

The Union Flag, also known as the Union Jack, is the national flag of the United Kingdom of Great Britain and Northern Ireland, and its dependant overseas territories. It was officially created by royal proclamation of King James I of England (James VI of Scotland) in 1606, as a unifying measure between the two formerly separate kingdoms. First featuring the red Cross of Saint George of England superimposed on the blue and white Saltire of Saint Andrew of Scotland, the current design with the offset red Saltire of St Patrick of Ireland was formally adopted in 1801. Being asymmetrical, the widest part of the white diagonal should be uppermost on the side closest to the flagpole. When flown inverted, formerly as a distress signal, it is considered offensive by some people. Strictly, the term Union Jack only applies when the flag is flown from the jack-staff of a ship of the Royal Navy. Unfortunately, many decorative versions of the Union Flag show it incorrectly as being either symmetrical in design and often, wrongly proportioned: it should be twice its height in length. The Union Flag is displayed as a proud symbol of all that is **Best of British**.

Union Flag:

Half-mast: When flown at half-mast, the flag should be at two-thirds of the way up the flagpole, with at least the height of the flag between it and the top of the pole.

Permission: Any individual or organisation, except for the Police Service of Northern Ireland (PSNI), can fly the Union Flag whenever they choose. No planning permission is required. The PSNI can only fly its service flag, or the Royal Standard during official visits by the Sovereign.